December 10, 1998   Just for Me.

SPENCER HART

CHARTWELL
BOOKS, INC.

Page 2 photograph:
Living room, Edwin H.
Cheney house, Oak Park,
Illinois.

Published by
CHARTWELL BOOKS, INC.
A division of BOOK SALES, INC.
114, Northfield Avenue
Edison, New Jersey 08837

Produced by
Saraband Inc, PO Box 0032, Rowayton, CT 06853-0032

Copyright © 1998, Saraband Inc.

Design © Ziga Design

ISBN 0-7858-0992-9

Printed in China

10 9 8 7 6 5 4 3 2 1

◨ FOR DONNA

CONTENTS

Wright Rooms

BY SPENCER HART

ore than a century has passed since Frank Lloyd Wright's birth in 1867, but interest in his work has never been higher. His uniquely personal vision of architecture and design bore fruit in hundreds of completed buildings, most of which still stand, and in countless beautiful drawings for unbuilt projects. His career spanned more than seventy years, from his employment as a draftsman in the Chicago office of Adler and Sullivan in 1887 until his death in 1959 at the age of ninety-two. Throughout that time, his views on what he called "organic architecture"—a style based on natural forms—were constantly evolving into new and unexpected dimensions. Tirelessly imaginative and creative, often difficult and demanding, he had the same answer for everyone who asked him which of his projects was his favorite: "The next one!"

Although he studied architecture and civil engineering for some time at the University of Wisconsin, Wright learned mainly by doing, his prodigious energy focused by several influences that remained paramount throughout his career. This book explores five aspects of the synthesis Wright created from those influences. The chapter

Above: Frank Lloyd
Wright at work in his
Wisconsin home/studio,
Taliesin, late in his career.

Page 6: South-facing
window wall of the
revolutionary Frederick C.
Robie house (1906),
designed for a narrow city
lot in Chicago. Note the
double-sided fireplace that
serves as a screen between
living and dining areas.

headings are drawn from his own voluminous writings on modern architecture and society, including his autobiography, first published in 1932 and revised several times in subsequent years.

The phrase "Vista, Breadth, Depth" suggests Wright's overriding concern with spatial unity and freedom—a determination to "break out of the box" created by traditional architecture and allow interior and exterior spaces to flow into one another. His buildings rose naturally from their sites and allowed their occupants to move freely between indoor and outdoor environments, between common areas for living and dining and private spaces for rest, work and relaxation. His turn-of-the-century Prairie Houses commanded immediate attention for their low, sweeping rooflines, wide sheltering eaves, continuous bands of windows, and expansive, asymmetrical forms. Even in an increasingly urban Midwest, they conveyed a sense of groundedness, shelter and informality intimately associated with country life.

Wright never lost his love for the rural Wisconsin landscape where he grew up, and, in fact, returned to it in 1911 to establish the hillside home and studio he called Taliesin ("shining brow"). The name recalled his Welsh ancestry through his mother's family, the Lloyd Joneses, who had settled Spring Green in the early 1800s. From his father's side, he inherited a deep love of music and a streak of New England Transcendentalism. His father, William Cary Wright, left the family before the children were grown—a pattern Wright would repeat in his first marriage. Taliesin became a refuge from the shock and disapproval that rocked the suburb of Oak Park, Illinois, when the rising young architect left his wife, Catherine Tobin, and their six children for the wife of a neighbor and client. By that time, he had already built or remodeled twenty-two houses in Oak Park, including his own innovative home and studio, and designed the famous Unity Temple for the Unitarian congregation, of which he was a member. The Oak Park houses represent some of his finest early work, undertaken during and after his employment by Louis Sullivan.

Sullivan's influence is apparent in several details of the Oak Park houses, including the Rollin Furbeck House of 1897, which has decorative plaster columns in the Sullivan style halfway up the three-story façade. They are richly ornamented in curvilinear forms abstracted from nature. Wright would use such natural forms consistently, but his abstractions became more and more geometric—triangles, squares, rectangles recurring as motifs in art glass, furniture, floor grids and other elements of his buildings. His preoccupation with form took him a step beyond Sullivan's statement that "form follows function": for Wright, form and function were one. This is clear from designs like that of the Darwin D. Martin House (1904) in Buffalo, New York. All the living spaces are rectilinear, and every feature repeats the same proportions, down to the Tree of Life design in the art-glass windows. Carla Lind makes an incisive comparison of Wright's ornamental style vis-à-vis Sullivan's in her book *Lost Wright* (Simon & Schuster, 1996). In describing the façade of Wright's Francisco Terrace Apartments, built in Chicago in 1895, she states:

Below: Detail from Louis Sullivan's landmark Wainwright Building in St. Louis, Missouri (1890–92), showing the ornamental terra-cotta window panels.

"The prevailing circular motif integral to the decorative composition is more graphic and modular than in Sullivan's work. Wrought-iron gates, no doubt manufactured by Wright's friend and client William Winslow, captured the spirit of Sullivan's terra-cotta patterns, but each of Wright's designs draws on the innate characteristics of the respective materials for its power. The wrought iron was more linear, the terra cotta more plastic. Tiny beadwork and custom handling of the extremely long Roman bricks created more ornament on the building's façade."

Wright's phrase "the House Beautiful" evokes his affinity with the nineteenth-century Arts and Crafts movement, with its deep respect for the beauty of natural materials and unpretentious, integrated design. Wherever possible, he designed all the furniture and fittings for his houses, in keeping with his credo of organic architecture. Most of his work was residential, comprising some 315 single-family houses, the majority of them in the Midwest, but with unique examples from Carmel, California, to lower New England. He was one of the first to perceive the potential inherent in well-made manufactured goods—a point on which he diverged from most other admirers of the Arts and Crafts ethic promulgated by England's William Morris in the 1850s and popularized by C.R. Ashbee. While Wright agreed with the movement's emphasis on "honest" materials and craftsmanship, he did not insist that only handmade goods were acceptable for "the House Beautiful" as envisioned by early Arts and Crafts enthusiasts. In fact, one of his earliest lectures (1901) was on "The Art and Craft of the Machine." In a radical departure from prevailing ideas on the subject, he stated: "Usurped by Greed and deserted by its natural interpreter, the Artist, the Machine is only the creature, not the creator of this inequity [shoddy mass-produced goods]. I say the Machine has noble possibilities unwillingly forced to this degradation, degraded by the Arts themselves."

Never one to mince words, he criticized American architecture sharply in the portfolio of his works published in Europe by Ernst Wasmuth in 1910: "Our better-class residences are chiefly tributes to English architecture, cut open inside and embellished to suit; porches and 'conveniences' added: the result in most cases a pitiful mongrel." He was deeply committed to the ideal of an indigenous American architecture that reflected the needs and aspirations of a democratic society. To this end, he worked to unify aesthetic and structure into a harmonious whole. Naturally, some clients were dismayed when he proposed to get rid of all of their existing furniture and accessories, but others gave him a free hand, and the results speak for themselves in designs like that of the Robie House, Fallingwater, the Dana-Thomas House and others described and illustrated on the following pages.

Some of the Arts and Crafts elements incorporated into Wright's early work include the use of patterned brickwork and smooth stucco over wood framing; fireplaces flanked by built-in seating, sometimes set into an alcove; mottoes inscribed on wall panels; lighting fixtures of copper and other metals, with flower-form or geometric shades; simple art pottery like that produced by the Grueby and Fulper studios, with green or earthtone glazes; informal arrangements of wayside flowers and grasses; and the use of wooden banding, or trim strips, to unite the wall and ceiling planes, giving human scale to even the largest rooms. The F.C. Bogk House in Milwaukee (1916) illustrates many of these features. There is a built-in bench at the fireplace with a table-arm at one end and a bookcase along the back, above the upholstered seating. Full-height French windows in the living room unite the house and its site. A wide trim strip with inset lighting near ceiling level is balanced by a narrow strip below, broken by the tall windows on two sides of the room. Rare examples of Wright-designed caned chairs were made for this house, and for the Sherman Booth House in Glencoe, Illinois (1915).

The Booth House, designed for Wright's lawyer Sherman W. Booth, was part of the Ravine Bluffs Development, which comprised five other houses commissioned by Booth as rentals. All six dwellings have plaster surfaces with wood trim, and the Booth House featured some notable furniture designs by Wright, including a wooden floor lamp derived from the Japanese print stands exhibited earlier at the Art Institute of Chicago.

The impressive Joseph W. Husser House overlooking Lake Michigan in Chicago (designed in 1899, and, unfortunately, demolished) looked toward the Prairie House style and had many Arts and Crafts features. Octagonal elements—like the library Wright designed for his Oak Park studio—appeared in the plan, and living quarters were raised several stories above ground level. The exterior frieze below the roofline, as well as the façade and window treatments, reflected the influence of Louis Sullivan. Design historians Kathryn B. Hiesinger and George H. Marcus provide valuable information about the interior appointments in their book *Landmarks of Twentieth Century Design* (Abbeville Press, 1993):

"With his dining room for the Joseph W. Husser house, Frank Lloyd Wright established the pattern of high-back slatted chairs and large tables with thick overhanging tops and massive legs ... exaggerated in scale like those of Charles Rennie Mackintosh. They were not designed as individual components, but as part of a total unit: the twenty-four chairs and three tables formed a regular, rhythmical pattern of geometric shapes, with the slatted bases on the table ends completing the composition." This theme recurs again and again in Wright's dining rooms on a smaller scale, creating the effect of a "room within a room." Some examples, like the dining room table of the Meyer May House in Grand Rapids, Michigan, have built-in ornamental lighting fixtures at the corners, which increase the sense of enclosure.

One of the last Prairie houses was Northome, designed for Francis W. Little in Deephaven, Minnesota, in 1912. Now demolished, this masterful design contained some of the oak furniture created for the first Little House in Peoria, Illinois (1903). Fortunately, two rooms from Northome have been preserved: the living room, reconstructed in the American wing of New York City's Metropolitan Museum of Art, and the library, rebuilt for the Allentown Art Museum in Pennsylvania. Wright historian Carla Lind has described the fifty-five-foot living room in *The Wright Style* (Simon & Schuster, 1992):

"The room's transition from a natural site to a museum setting has refocused the perception of this space as an art object. Still compelling are the linear power of the light screens, the mastery of scale and proportion, the delicate strength of the wood spindles, the subtle contrasts in color and pattern, the variety and unity within the space."

Wright was not only a superb draftsman, as seen from his renderings, elevations and detailed sketches; his innate sense of color and form pervaded his buildings, as suggested by the phrase "the Riches, the Materials." Wright rooms are studies in burnished woods, warm brick tones, rugged stonework, elegant fabrics, subtle lighting and masterful art glass that carries out the color scheme implicit in the presentation drawings. Every object contributes to the ambience. In *Frank Lloyd Wright Interiors and Furniture* (Academy

Below: The elegant David B. Gamble house in Pasadena, designed by the Arts and Crafts architects Charles Sumner Greene and his brother Henry Mather Greene, in 1908. Note the hand-carved woodwork and fireplace surround of ceramic tile.

Below: Recessed skylight above the massive fireplace with concrete relief in the Aline Barnsdall house, Los Angeles (1923).

Group Ltd., 1994), architect and historian Thomas A. Heinz gives us an example in his description of a rug designed in 1909 for the Avery Coonley House in Riverside, Illinois:

"The rug colours reflected the colours of the house. The border paralleled the woodwork colour. The sheepskin beige of the centre matched the colour of the ceiling plaster throughout the house. The olive green squares are the same colour as the plaster on the walls in the living room and adjacent halls….The bright lime green is the exact colour of the cathedral glass in the art glass windows."

Wright's unerring eye for combining color and texture is most apparent in the houses that he designed from the ground up for appreciative clients with generous budgets. One of the best-known examples is the Frederick C. Robie House, which has been referred to as "the house of the century." Now owned by the University of Chicago, it is one of the seventeen buildings designated by the American Institute of Architects to be retained as an example of Wright's architectural contribution to American culture. Designed for a wealthy young inventor in 1906, its innovative features include a massive, two-sided sunken fireplace that serves as a screen between living and dining areas; a continuous band of art-glass doors along the south façade of this common area; and Wright-designed rugs that unify the long rectangular sweep of space.

Certain colors recur frequently in Wright's work, most of them drawn from nature: the rich golds of sunlight, autumn and prairie-grass seedheads; the olive green of various trees and wayside plants; the soothing muted tones of winter landscapes; and bright splashes of pumpkin orange, cerulean blue and Cherokee red (Wright's favorite color, used for his signature block). Both inside and out, color is used to define and highlight form, or drawn into the composition from the surrounding landscape. This is in keeping with

the principles of Japanese art and architecture, which had a profound influence on Wright and is discussed more fully in chapter 5.

Stained and leaded glass were extremely popular with early exponents of the Arts and Crafts school, and Wright took the demanding medium of art glass to new heights with the help of skilled glaziers at the Luxfer Prism and Linden Glass Companies, who transformed his designs into skylights, windows, French doors, cabinet doors and light fixtures. During the early twentieth century, leading European designers like Koloman Moser and Josef Hoffmann of Vienna's Wiener Werkstätte admired Wright's work deeply and favored geometric designs like those he used. The brilliant young German designer Josef Olbrich, a cofounder of the Secessionist movement, may well have influenced Wright through such international publications as Munich's *Jugend* and the Parisian *La Revue Blanche*, as well as the widely read *Studio* magazine. In fact, when Wright visited Europe in 1910, he was somewhat chagrined to hear himself described as "the American Olbrich." He always resisted comparison to other architects, including some of those who had worked with him and went on to practice what was called Prairie School architecture.

American architects and designers who acknowledged their debt to Wright included Paul T. Frankl, a native of Vienna who opened a gallery in New York in 1914. There, during the 1920s, he first sold his "skyscraper" furniture — wooden cabinetry with stepped silhouettes and sharp angles like those of Manhattan's office towers. According to *Landmarks of Twentieth Century Design*, "His work was considered thoroughly modern and purely American." In 1928 he dedicated his book *New Dimensions* to Wright.

Some of Wright's most impressive examples of textured materials occur in the concrete-block houses designed for California clients during the 1920s. They include the Alice Madison Millard House, La Miniatura, at Pasadena (1923), and the larger houses designed for clients John Storer, Samuel Freeman and Charles Ennis in Los Angeles. The "textile blocks" used to build these houses were patterned in molds of Wright's design. Some of them are solid, others pierced to admit light. Laid up into walls, they produce an effect much like that of a Mayan temple. Since the blocks are patterned on both sides, the interiors are richly textured, apart from furnishings and fixtures.

"At Work in Stone" speaks to Wright's affinity for masonry, whether expressed in brick, stone, terra cotta, concrete blocks, poured concrete, or a combination of these materials. He experimented endlessly with their possibilities, which were perhaps uniquely suited to his need to build lasting structures. Much of Wright's best early work was done in narrow Roman brick, sometimes in alternating courses that resembled board-and-batten construction, in which narrow strips of wood alternate with wider ones. Most of the brick in the early houses was in warm brown or gold tones, rather than the traditional red.

While brick and stone are the most labor-intensive construction materials, their durability and resistance to fire are strong recommendations. And, where available near the building site, they are consistent with the Arts and Crafts commitment to vernacular architecture, as expressed by the influential furniture maker Gustav Stickley in his 1911 publication *More Craftsman Homes*: "A house that is built of stone where stones are in the fields, of concrete where the soil is sandy, of brick where brick can be had reasonably, or of wood if the house is in a mountainous, wooded region, will from the beginning belong to the landscape."

Some of Wright's most impressive masonry designs are for the fireplaces and chimneys that he defined as "the heart of the house." His Oak Park home and studio have several examples, including the inglenook fireplace of Roman brick in the living room

Above: *Wrought-iron grillework frames a view of the plain and patterned textile blocks laid up in two-story columns for the Charles Ennis house, built on a ridge of the Santa Monica Mountains overlooking Los Angeles.*

and the monochromatic brick fireplace with piers in the studio drafting room. Both have arched openings with fan-shaped surrounds, a pattern that recurs in many of his early entrances. It suggests the influence of Henry Hobson Richardson, the Louisiana-born architect who initiated the Romanesque revival in the United States and broke ground for the movement toward an indigenous modern architecture.

Wright's brick firepace for the William E. Martin House in Oak Park (1902) has a long rectangular opening flanked by piers, with built-in seating and bookcases to one side. It is the focal point of the spacious living room, and its massive chimney pierces the hipped roof in the style characteristic of the Prairie houses. It was two years later that Wright designed the handsome horizontal house of gold-toned Roman brick for the client's brother, Darwin D. Martin, in Buffalo, New York. Low walls and piers capped by concrete coping extend from the house to link it wih the grounds. Some of the piers bear the large shallow pedestal urns that appear in so many of the early Prairie houses. Like the concrete footing that extended from the base of his exterior walls, they were a Wright design signature.

The California concrete-block houses of the 1920s have been mentioned as reminiscent of pre-Columbian architecture. Another notable example is the massive Mayan-looking house built for the actress and art patroness Aline Barnsdall between 1916 and 1920. Poured concrete is the primary construction material. It is often called Hollyhock House, for the abstracted flower design used as an ornamental motif throughout. Built on Olive Hill (now Barnsdall Park), overlooking Los Angeles, it is atypical of Wright's work in presenting a closed façade that dominates the surrounding landscape: It looks inward to a broad patio and luxuriously appointed rooms with touches of Oriental splendor. (During this period, Wright spent much of his time in Japan, working on the Imperial Hotel commission.) His associate Rudolf Schindler supervised construction of the Studio Residence on the property and later designed the furniture for the Freeman House (1923).

The Imperial Hotel in Tokyo (demolished 1968) was a unique essay in masonry using soft native lava stone, called oya, combined with brick. The lava stone was readily carved into ornate columns, cornices, free-standing sculptures and ornaments for the reflecting pool and a series of garden courtyards. More than 700 drawings were involved in this project, for which Wright designed all the furniture, murals, tableware, linen, silver, glass, upholstery fabrics and carpets, which were woven in China to his specifications. Originally proposed in 1913, the hotel occupied much of Wright's time for the next eight years. Due to his careful planning, it survived the violent earthquake of 1923, but ultimately fell to the high prices of Tokyo real estate. The entrance and multilevel lobby were reconstructed at Meiji Mura Park, in Nagoya.

Wright's Wisconsin home and studio, Taliesin, suffered several disastrous fires, but rebuilding and expansion continued. It would evolve into one of the world's best-known private residences. Native limestone, combined with timber and plaster surfacing, is its primary construction material. Stone walls, piers and fireplaces were constructed to resemble the natural outcroppings of the limestone, and the plan is spacious and informal, with the look of an Oriental compound. Wright's last sketch was for the garden at Taliesin, built for his third wife, Olgivanna Milanov, in 1959, the year that he died. By that time, Taliesin had long since grown to include the former Hillside Home School, designed for Wright's aunts in 1901 and converted to use by the newly founded Taliesin Fellowship of apprentice architects in the early 1930s.

In 1937 members of the Fellowship would begin work on the winter home/studio, Taliesin West, near Scottsdale, Arizona. This innovative structure of desert rubblestone, concrete, redwood and canvas was designed to afford protection from the glaring light and heat of Maricopa Mesa, from which it appears to rise like a feature of the landscape. Subsequent remodelings and additions introduced more weatherproof roofing materials and other improvements while remaining faithful to the original triangular form — a long, low axis slashed by diagonal supporting members.

The early 1930s brought few commissions on account of the Great Depression, and Wright focused on lecturing and writing to generate income and promulgate his ideas. His Utopian views on decentralized city planning and affordable, livable modern homes took shape in the 12-foot-by-12-foot model called Broadacre City, built for the 1935 Industrial Arts Exhibition at New York's Rockefeller Center. One of its primary concepts was that of the Usonian House (Wright's acronym for United States of North America), which was first executed for Herbert and Katherine Jacobs in Madison, Wisconsin, in 1936. The couple did much of the work themselves to keep costs low, and the house was built for some $5,500. Set upon a concrete slab in which heating coils had been embedded in gravel, its brick wall masses carry most of the supports for the flat roof. The remaining walls are of prefabricated wood and insulated plywood inset with glass doors. Bands of clerestory windows increase the available light, and the house faces the sloping garden behind it, rather than the street side, for privacy. Variations on this basic design would be adapted to sites across the nation during the remainder of Wright's career.

Probably, Wright's best-known and most admired work in masonry is the house he named Fallingwater (1936), built for Edgar J. Kaufmann, Sr., in Mill Run, Pennsylvania. Its primary materials are cantilevered concrete, native sandstone and glass. The sandstone walls were laid up in rugged alternating courses that contrast with the smooth multilevel terraces of reinforced concrete that soar out from the solid rock in which they are anchored. The huge living room is floored with flagstone, and the glazed south-facing wall has a view of the highland stream, Bear Run, over which the house is poised. Five years later, Wright designed a handsome guest house and walkway, with a stepped concrete canopy, for the property. Fallingwater has been owned by the Western Pennsylvania Conservancy since 1963. It was the gift of architect Edgar J. Kaufmann, Jr., a former apprentice at Taliesin who introduced Wright to his father.

Below: The prairie sumac motif was reprised in dozens of variations for the incomparable art glass of the thirty-five-room Dana-Thomas house in Springfield, Illinois (1902).

Another memorable project of the 1930s is the Herbert F. Johnson House, Wingspread, designed in 1937 for the Wisconsin client who had commissioned the Johnson Wax Company complex, a landmark in commercial architecture, the previous year. Built on a former nature preserve in Wind Point, Wisconsin, Wingspread has been described by Wright historian William Allin Storrer as "the last of the Prairie houses. Its pinwheel plan is zoned—that is, sleeping quarters are in [one] wing, kitchen in the opposite and so forth. This pinwheel, as Wright employs it, a simple variant of his favorite cruciform plan, extends from a central, three-story-high octagon....Wright considered this his most expensive and best-built house to date" (*The Architecture of Frank Lloyd Wright: A Complete Catalog*, MIT Press). The primary construction materials are mellow red brick, pink Kasota sandstone and cypress.

Wright's first work in northern California was the Paul R. Hanna House in Stanford (1936), known as Honeycomb House for the hexagonal grid on which it was based.

Built of San Jose brick, glass and wood, this Usonian design provided for maximum flexibility of interior space through the easy disassembly and repositioning of nonmasonry walls. Both courtyards and interior afford a warm, welcoming environment enhanced by the use of redwood paneling and extension of the sunken hearth into the living area as a shallow, terraced brick enclave capped with darker brick. After the Hannas deeded the house to Stanford University, where Professor Paul Hanna was a faculty member, in 1974, the Nissan Motor Company contributed substantially to its endowment in appreciation for Wright's lifelong interest in Japanese culture.

Wright's commitment to a "Living Sympathy with Nature" was deeply influenced by his feeling for Japanese art and architecture. Even before the Imperial Hotel commission, he had traveled to Japan, collected Japanese prints and incorporated Oriental elements into designs for buildings and furniture. The Arts and Crafts movement had embraced this aesthetic in many forms, including ebonized and lacquered furniture; art pottery featuring lotus flowers, chrysanthemums and exotic birds; and—most specific to Wright's work—asymmetrical designs that evoked universal principles without sacrificing the power of individuality. As Isabelle Anscombe points out in *Arts & Crafts Style*

(Phaidon Press, 1991): "Oriental art tended to blur the distinctions between the fine and applied arts…. Artists struggling to escape from the strict demarcations set by the [British] Royal Academy found in Japanese arts not only a welcome simplicity and new forms of representation, but also an ancient respect for other media."

A look at the characteristics of the basic Japanese folkhouse reveals many parallels with Wright's work, including small windows covered by rhythmic wooden grilles; bold, geometric structural forms; flexible, translucent screens in place of interior walls; free-standing houses with their own compounds and gardens, rather than attached dwellings; and large sheltering roofs. Architectural photographer and writer Norman F. Carver, Jr., has preserved many of these rapidly vanishing structures in his book *Japanese Folkhouses* (Documan Press, 1984), in which he states that the historic Shinto shrine at Ise, "combining the Shinto veneration of nature with the Japanese preference for simple, straight lines…firmly established the integration of natural and geometric form—which eventually became the hallmark of all Japanese architecture."

Wright's exposure to Eastern art and culture may have begun with his employment by architect Joseph Lyman Silsbee in 1887. Silsbee had moved to Chicago from the eastern seaboard to become part of the architectural renaissance that succeeded the devastating Chicago fire of 1871. He collected Orientalia and designed in the vernacular Shingle style that Wright used for his first home studio. During his employment with Adler & Sullivan, Wright worked on the commission for the Transportation Building at the World's Columbian Exposition (1893), where Japanese culture was represented by a half-scale replica of a temple from the Fujiwara period. He often used Oriental artworks in his designs, including the complex at Taliesin, and carried out three other commissions in Japan while working on the Imperial Hotel—two private houses and a girls' school.

In the first edition of his autobiography, which revitalized interest in his work in 1932, Wright restated his thesis that "pure design is abstraction of nature-elements in purely geometric terms." As the stark International Style of the European Modernists gained ground over the next twenty-five years, Wright steadily opposed their high-rise glass-and-steel towers carried on structural piers (*pilotes*) of reinforced concrete. While conceding reluctantly that the skyscraper was fundamental to American architecture, he still envisioned it as a free-standing structure widely dispersed among parklike settings in his ideal, decentralized city of the future.

Toward the end of his life, Wright's designs became even more organic and sculptural, as seen in the circular house he created for his son David Wright in Phoenix, Arizona (1950) and the solar hemicycle for his youngest son, Robert Llewellyn Wright, in Bethesda, Maryland (1953). Perhaps the best-known, and most controversial, of his postwar buildings is the Solomon R. Guggenheim Museum in New York City, completed in 1956. This expanding spiral of sprayed and poured concrete combines structural and spatial principles toward which Wright had worked throughout his seventy-five-year career. It seems likely that he would have agreed with the assessment of the contemporary scene offered by Norman F. Carver, Jr., in *Japanese Folkhouses*:

"At a time when architecture appears lost in the self-indulgent and irrelevant aesthetic play of 'post-modernism,' my studies have convinced me that vernacular architecture…provides desperately needed insights into the fundamental connections between man, society, nature, and architecture."

Vista, Breadth, Depth

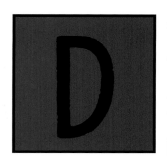avid A. Hanks observed in his perceptive study *The Decorative Designs of Frank Lloyd Wright* (E.P. Dutton, 1979) that "Wherever one happens to be in a Wright house seems to be the center, because the spaces give the uncanny impression of adjusting themselves to the viewer, somehow appearing to be custom-made for the moment.... A similar effect is created by his furnishings."

The grammar of Wright's unique spatial language has been studied by many architectural historians, including those who worked with him over the years. Each has something to contribute, as does Wright himself in his many books, articles and lectures. Of course, the best way to experience a Wright house is from the inside out, as a design for living. But the pictures that follow have much to tell us about the unity and harmony of the Wright room.

One element that contributed to Wright's feeling for space and volume was the set of Froebel "gift blocks" he received as a child. They were designed by Friedrich Froebel, the German pioneer of early-childhood education, during the 1830s to teach children about geometric form. The wooden blocks were of many shapes, not only

Above: Shingled façade of the Frank Lloyd Wright Home and Studio in Oak Park (1889-1909), with the octagonal library, at left, marked by its massive chimney.

Page 18: Entrance hall to the P.A. Beachy House in Oak Park (1906), with second-floor screening that soars above the long cushioned bench between wooden piers.

cubes, but triangles, rectangles, spheres, cylinders. They could be recombined endlessly into houses, barns, bridges and other imaginative creations. In his autobiography, Wright spoke of his debt to Froebel when he wrote: "The maple-wood blocks…all are in my fingers to this day."

Another major influence was Wright's mentor Louis Sullivan, whom he always referred to with deep respect, even during the many years that they were estranged. During his early twenties, Wright spent six years working for Sullivan and his partner Dankmar Adler in their thriving Chicago practice. When Wright designed the entire January 1938 issue of *Architectural Forum*, fourteen years after Sullivan's death, he dedicated it to "my beloved master Louis Henry Sullivan and grand old chief Dankmar Adler."

Regarded as the spiritual father of modern architecture, Sullivan was an outspoken critic of the imitation of historic styles that dominated the architecture of his time. Although he had studied at the revered *École des Beaux Arts* in Paris, he looked to a new style that expressed modern functional needs. He was a pioneer in the aesthetics of early skyscraper design and upheld the principle of an organic architecture based on natural forms. His most memorable works include Chicago's Carson Pirie Scott department store and Auditorium Building, and the Wainwright Building in St. Louis.

Wright worked with Sullivan on the innovative Transportation Building for the 1893 Columbian Exposition, held in Chicago, and gradually assumed many of Adler and Sullivan's residential commissions. Sullivan's genius for ornamentation was expressed in the great Golden Door for the Transportation Building, and in the naturalistic reliefs and colored stencil patterns of the Auditorium Building. His influence is also apparent in Wright's Oak Park Home and Studio, a laboratory for artistic experiments carried out before and after Wright's 1893 break with his mentor. (They quarreled about what Wright called his "bootlegged houses"— the buildings he designed on his own account in violation of his contract with Sullivan's firm. Both were volatile men of strong feelings, and Wright was fired.)

Sullivan's exuberant curvilinear forms, based on natural motifs like flowers and foliage, appear in early Wright designs like the exterior frieze and interior arcade of the William Winslow House (1894), in River Forest, Illinois. However, over time Wright's designs became more abstract and geometric. As David A. Hanks points out: "Wright felt that Sullivan had not realized his true goal of an organic architecture….[He] did believe that in the 'plasticity' and 'living intricacy' of Sullivan's terra-cotta ornament, the background vanished so that the material and the ornament were unified….He did not believe, however, that organic ornament made an organic architecture." Thus he moved on to simpler forms that could be machine-made in ways that were faithful to the nature of the various materials.

Two features of Wright's early houses worked to define space and scale in new ways: wooden moldings (also called stripping, or stringcourses) and window glass. Both of these elements are prominent in pre-Prairie houses like the one designed for Oak Park neighbor Nathan G. Moore in 1895 and the now-demolished Joseph Husser residence (1899) in Chicago. They are fully realized in such masterful Prairie houses as Chicago's Frederick C. Robie residence (1906) and the Avery Coonley house and Playhouse (1907 and 1912) in Riverside, Illinois. In these examples, and many others, the wooden moldings work to unify and define the spacious living areas and bring human scale to the inner environment. They are seamlessly interwoven with lighting fixtures, skylights and bands of art-glass windows and French doors that function as "light screens" to provide color, warmth and privacy—a pre-eminent feature of Wright residential designs. Both moldings and movable partitions in place of fixed walls were fixtures of Japanese architecture and had

Below: The California "textile-block" house designed for John Storer in 1923, using rectilinear forms and machine-made materials. Three generations of Wright architects have worked on this building, including Wright's son Lloyd Wright, who supervised its construction, and his grandson Eric Wright, who restored it in association with Joel Silver during the 1980s.

Above: *The spacious, stone-flagged living area in the landmark house Fallingwater, which rises above the stream called Mill Run in western Pennsylvania. It was designed for Edgar J. Kaufmann, Sr., in 1935. This view shows the simplicity Wright believed was possible when all elements combine to make a coherent whole.*

been reinterpreted by American Shingle-style architects like Joseph Lyman Silsbee, for whom Wright worked briefly in 1887. The influence of Oriental art and architecture on Wright's work is discussed more fully in chapters 2 and 5.

Early in his career, Wright designed many Prairie-style furnishings tailored to his unique interiors. Most of these pieces were of quarter-sawn oak, often stained in natural shades to co-ordinate with the moldings. Built-in furniture and fixtures were uniquely appropriate to his interiors, as they worked in the cause of unity. His early pieces included sideboards, bookcases, benches, settees and breakfronts—cabinets with a projecting central section. Many of these fixtures had art-glass doors in patterns that harmonized with window designs. Movable furniture included heavy, usually rectangular, dining room tables, with tall chairs having slatted or spindled backs. They created a sense of enclosure within the dining area itself. Much of this and other furniture made to his specifications was crafted by reliable suppliers like John W. Ayers of Chicago and Milwaukee's Matthews Bros. Furniture Company, which employed several hundred skilled German cabinet makers.

Simplicity was Wright's watchword in furniture design, and in his autobiography he distinguished between his approach and that of other well-known designers of the time. As always, his opinions were not understated:

"Plainness was not necessarily simplicity….Crude furniture of the Roycroft-Stickley-Mission style…was offensively plain, plain as a barn-door—but never simple in any true sense. Nor, I found, were merely machine-made things in themselves necessarily simple….I believe that no one thing in itself is ever so, but must achieve simplicity…as a perfectly realized part of some organic whole."

It is unfortunate that so many of Wright's early landscape designs, which were wholly integrated with his houses, have disappeared over time. These "garden rooms" flowed out from terraces, balconies and semiconcealed entrances to extend the living space into the environment. A notable example is that of the grounds for the Darwin D. Martin House in Buffalo, New York (1904). The generous budget for this project made it Wright's most ambitious house to that date, with a hundred-foot gallery enclosed by glass opening to a conservatory, plus stable, garage and gardener's cottage. Fortunately, the Darwin house, owned by the State University of New York at Buffalo for thirty years, has recently undergone admirable restoration work.

In some cases, Wright entrusted landscape design to gifted colleagues like Walter Burley Griffin, who planned the beautiful grounds for Darwin D. Martin's brother, William E. Martin, in Oak Park (1903). They included several gardens, pools, a pergola and a lawn tennis court.

Horizontality was the keynote of these Prairie house designs, as observed by Mary Hollingsworth in *Architecture of the 20th Century* (Brompton Books, 1988): "[Wright's] early buildings made important innovations in the development of the ground plan, already anticipated in the private commissions of McKim, Mead and White, and the synthesis of the plan with the elevation. His emphasis on horizontality is similar to that of Charles Voysey" (a British architect of the Arts and Crafts movement, whose work Wright admired). The influence of the Arts and Crafts movement on Wright's work is discussed in the following chapter.

Even as he turned in new directions after his return from Europe in 1911, Wright held his vision of "Vista, Breadth, Depth," in contrast to other exponents of modern architecture in both Europe and the United States. In discussing the decades between 1920 and 1960, Dorothy Spencer points out, in *Total Design: Objects by Architects* (Chronicle Books, 1991), that "Modernism in the United States had been dominated by European architects, with the exception of Frank Lloyd Wright." By the 1940s, Wright's buildings were based on "single geometric forms such as triangles and arcs. His subsequent projects consisted of repeated modular units such as triangles, hexagons and circles." These Usonian houses of his later career, far from being cold and inhuman in scale, were eminently livable and as closely linked to their surroundings as his original designs. They stood for his ideal of a non-elite American architecture tailored to individual needs and consistent with life in a democratic society.

Below: The triangular metal grid above the drafting room of the Taliesin Fellowship complex (Hillside) suggests the tools of the architect's trade. This 1932 remodeling of Wright's earlier Hillside Home School was made for the use of apprentices at his home/studio in Spring Green, Wisconsin.

True to form, Wright attacked the impersonality of the International Style in a series of lectures given at Princeton University in 1930, notably "The Cardboard House." As Hollingsworth reports: "Starting with the anthropomorphic view of the house, likening electric wiring to the nervous system and plumbing to the digestive system, he criticized modern architecture on the grounds that it did not take the organic nature of architecture into consideration, but sought to impose universal solutions. He rather frivolously suggested that they should trim all the trees to match!"

回 DIGNITY AND SERENITY

Edwin H. Cheney House (1903), Oak Park, Ill.

Opposite and below: It is hard to believe that this self-contained house, which looks so contemporary, was designed at the turn of the century. In the living room, oak moldings, the built-in bookcase and the ribbed vaulted ceiling define the area and keep it to human scale. Lamps and lighting fixtures harmonize with the iridescent art-glass windows (the house has fifty-two of them) for subdued lighting infused with color.

◐ A GRACIOUS WELCOME

Frank Lloyd Wright Home and Studio (1889-1909), Oak Park, Ill.

Opposite and above: Wright added this handsome studio to his home in 1895 for his architectural practice. The view of the foyer on the opposite page shows how the wooden piers work with other structural components to create a space that unfolds before the viewer, leading the eye into the drafting room beyond. Recessed lighting behind the ornamental ceiling grilles adds warmth to the burnished woodwork and textured walls. Above, another view of the built-in storage unit, surmounted by casement windows that frame the Sullivanesque ornamentation on the adjacent terrace.

◨ "THE HOUSE OF THE CENTURY"

Frederick C. Robie House (1906), Chicago, Ill.

Right: In 1958 *House and Home* magazine praised this exemplary Prairie house as a unique contribution to modern architecture. This view of the living area shows the continuous band of art-glass French doors that extends beyond the two-sided fireplace into the dining area. Wright designed all of the furniture and fittings, which were co-ordinated by the Milwaukee firm of Niedecken-Walbridge. Moldings and window mullions merge to frame an interior of rare spaciousness and livability.

Overleaf: A view of the prowlike bay in the living area, which has its counterpart at the other end of the main floor. The cantilevered arms of the couch serve as tables.

▣ VARIATIONS ON A THEME OF FOUR DECADES

Melvyn Maxwell Smith House (1946), Bloomfield Hills, Mich.; Frederick C. Robie House (1906)

Opposite and below: The commonalities between the Smith House on the opposite page and the Robie House below (view from chimney core into dining area) span a period of forty years. They include a fireplace that acts as both focal point and screen for the living/dining areas; glazed walls giving onto outdoor living space; respectful use of brick, wood and other materials; and simple geometric furnishings that are of, not "in," the free-flowing grid. Familiar Wright design signatures in the Smith House include natural pottery and sculpture, and clerestory light sources whose patterned effect is achieved by perforated wooden screens rather than the art glass of earlier years.

▣ ROOM WITHIN A ROOM

Ward W. Willits House (1901), Highland Park, Ill.
Right: The elegant Willits house dining room, with high-backed chairs creating an enclave around the rectangular table, has the "quiet streamline effects" that Wright considered essential to organic architecture. The Willits house is one of the seventeen Wright-designed buildings designated by the American Institute of Architects to be retained as an example of his architectural contribution to American culture.

◙ THE HORIZONTAL MODE
Prairie Houses, Oak Park, Ill.

Left: The Peter A. Beachy house (1906) was a complete remodeling that incorporated an earlier Victorian house into its structure. The new treatment was horizontal, an effect enhanced by the twin bands of molding — at and below ceiling level; the wide brick fireplace surround, with a low hearth framed by bands of stonework; and the twin upholstered couches with table-arms projecting over built-in shelving.

Above: The Harry S. Adams house (1913) was the last of twenty-three Oak Park buildings designed by Wright. This view from the dining room through the hall gives a sense of the seventy-foot vista of the ground-floor plan. Wooden stripping defines the roughly textured wall and ceiling planes, and the high-backed slatted chairs introduce a contrapuntal vertical note.

◨ WRIGHT RENAISSANCE
The Herbert F. Johnson House, "Wingspread" (1937)
Wind Point, Wisc.

Opposite and above: After a long period of frustration due to the Great Depression, Wright began a whole new career in his sixties, with a series of commissions that brought him to new creative heights. Of Wingspread, he said: "This is probably one of the most complete, best constructed and most expensive houses it has ever been my good fortune to build." The house forms a great pinwheel that extends from the massive three-story chimney (opposite). This brick core rises thirty feet through tiers of clerestory windows to a rooftop observatory. The huge octagonal living space comprises five areas, each with its own fireplace, defined by shallow steps and ceiling height rather than by walls.

▣ TEXTILE BUILDING BLOCKS

The John Storer House (1923), Hollywood, Calif.

Opposite and above: Wright was always fascinated by the possibilities inherent in the humble concrete block, which he called "the cheapest (and ugliest) thing in the building world." With this unpromising material, he built four of his richest-looking houses in California during the 1920s. The Storer House combined patterned and pierced blocks, precast in molds of Wright's design and laid up in bold columns and horizontals. Glazed walls give this elegant two-story living area, with terraces at either end, an incomparable view of Los Angeles. The original furniture was designed by Rudolf Schindler; the present owner has furnished the house from his extensive collection of Arts and Crafts objects.

◫ HEWED FROM NATIVE STONE

The Edgar J. Kaufmann, Sr., House
"Fallingwater" (1935), Mill Run, Penn.

Above and opposite: The huge square living room of
Fallingwater rises from the rock ledges that anchor the
house, which are reprised in the rough walls and piers of
native sandstone. The south façade has glazed walls overlooking the stream and the cantilevered balconies.
Shallow steps descend from the living room directly to
the plunge pool below it. Much of the informal furniture
is built in, including the long padded bench (opposite)
below the windows. Free-standing walnut furniture was
made to order in Milwaukee by Gillen Woodworking
Company, supervised by Taliesin apprentice Edgar Tafel.
According to David A. Hanks, "North Carolina walnut
and walnut veneer, selected for its variety in beautiful
graining, were used throughout the house."

THE HOUSE BEAUTIFUL

ARTS AND CRAFTS ELEMENTS

s the Arts and Crafts movement spread from Great Britain to Europe and the United States, it took on new forms of national and regional expression. It became an influence on American architects and artisans during the 1870s, when rigid historicism was yielding to demands for a new, more contemporary, style that retained the best of the past but shaped it by the principles of functionalism and simplicity. Arts and Crafts philosophy had been instrumental in this trend, which "rediscovered" native materials for fashioning decorative objects of wood, clay, metal, glass, leather and textiles.

A broad spectrum of American women had always been active in producing handicrafts for the home, either of necessity, or to fill their leisure time in creative ways. During the late nineteenth century, women experimented with the floral motifs of William Morris, the asymmetrical beauty of the Japanese style and regional innovations in ceramics, which inspired a flourishing art-pottery industry. And they became devoted readers of the emergent homemaking magazines, which were filled with ideas on improving the house and garden along Arts and Crafts lines. One of the most influential of these

Right: *The Hills-DeCaro house in Oak Park was a total remodeling of an earlier Victorian structure. Peaked rooflines with banded shingling and new casement windows helped change the emphasis to the horizontal.*

Page 44: *The inglenook fireplace with motto above was a familiar Arts and Crafts feature, seen here in the living room of Wright's house in Oak Park.*

magazines was the Curtis Publishing Company's *Ladies' Home Journal*, which brought Wright's ideas on architecture to national attention in 1901.

The first Wright design to appear in *The Ladies' Home Journal* was "A Home in a Prairie Town"—a graceful rendering of a house with horizontal lines and tiers of shallow hipped roofs overhanging casement windows. It was designed to be built for some $7,000 from plans that could be purchased from the magazine by mail. Within the next few years, several more designs by Wright were enthusiastically received by *Journal* readers, including "A Small House with Lots of Room in It" and a plan for an affordable fireproof house that was partly prefabricated. This exposure made Wright's work widely known and promulgated the Arts and Crafts ideals that had inspired him: the home as the stronghold of family life, focused around the hearth and unified by a sense of spaciousness, privacy and repose.

Despite the fact that most of his clients at the time were wealthy Chicago businessmen, Wright maintained a lifelong commitment to livable architecture for people of modest means, as seen in his later Usonian designs, the twelve-by-twelve-foot model for Broadacre City (analogous to the early Garden Cities envisioned by British architects) and his experiments in various forms of prefabrication from inexpensive materials.

As mentioned earlier, Wright usually urged his clients to furnish their houses with objects and fixtures of his own design, and the plates that follow show how effectively

THE CRAFTSMAN
VOL. V   FEBRUARY 1904   NO. 5

COPY 25 CENTS   PUBLISHED MONTHLY BY THE UNITED CRAFTS SYRACUSE·N·Y·–U·S·A·   YEAR 3 DOLLARS

Arts and Crafts elements function in these interiors. Native flowers, grasses and other plant forms inspired lamps and lighting fixtures with subtly colored shades of glass on metal bases. Door and window hardware, fire irons, ornamental grillework and other accessories were made to Wright's specifications by his friend William H. Winslow, whose Chicago firm developed iron and bronze casting processes used to produce metalwork for architects all over the country. Another early supplier was the Van Dorn Iron Works Company of Cleveland, Ohio, which advertised in *The Architectural Record*.

Wright, in turn, designed for metal craftsmen, including James A Miller, whom he described in his 1928 article "In the Cause of Architecture" as "a sheet-metal worker of Chicago, who had intelligent pride in his material and a sentiment concerning it....I designed some sheet copper bowls, slender flower holders and such things for him, and fell in love with sheet copper as a building material." It was objects like these that Wright used to furnish his several home/studios and many other interiors.

There are many parallels between the furniture Wright designed and that of Glasgow's Charles Rennie Mackintosh, another pioneer of the modern movement. One similarity is evident in Alan Crawford's comments in *Charles Rennie Mackintosh* (Thames and Hudson, 1995): "Most of his furniture was designed for particular rooms, of which he was often also the designer.... Move a Mackintosh chair in a Mackintosh interior, one might almost say, and you alter the whole ensemble."

Despite the fact that Wright became an outspoken critic of Gustav Stickley's Craftsman furniture, others have found it highly compatible with Wright rooms. Stickley trained as both a furniture maker and a stonemason, and he organized his successful turn-of-the-century enterprise along the lines of C.R. Ashbee's British Guild of Handicraft. He began publishing his influential magazine *The Craftsman* in 1901, not only to publicize his house and furniture designs, but to spread the Arts

Left: Gustav Stickley's magazine The Craftsman *promoted such Arts and Crafts ideals as unpretentious design and honest workmanship. It also advertised and showcased Stickley's furniture and houses, which were very popular in the early 1900s.*

Left: The Woodpecker *tapestry was designed by William Morris and woven at Morris & Company, Merton Abbey, in 1881. Like Morris, Wright drew inspiration from nature for his designs, colors and materials, but his designs soon became more geometric than curvilinear.*

and Crafts gospel in the United States. Neither Stickley nor Wright would go over to the Art Nouveau aesthetic that branched off from the Arts and Crafts movement in Europe during the late 1890s.

L'Art Nouveau took its name from art dealer Siegfried Bing's international art gallery, which opened in Paris in 1895. It featured interiors and furniture by Belgian architect Henry van der Velde, glassware by American designer Louis Comfort Tiffany, jewelry by the French designer René Lalique and decorative objects by Mackintosh himself. All of these luxurious wares were characterized by highly ornate and curvilinear forms derived largely from nature and were displayed at the Parisian *Exposition Universelle* in 1900.

As usual, Wright went his own way, "disassembling" such forms into their geometric components to make them an integral part of his buildings. Gustav Stickley, too, pursued his craftsmanship ideals until 1916, when mass-produced copies of his work at cheaper prices closed his business. At the same time, Louis C. Tiffany enjoyed acclaim for his elegant glassware, ceramics, lamps and leaded-glass landscape windows. According to an 1883 article in *Artistic Houses*, Tiffany's apartment on New York's East 23rd Street "combined all the hallmarks of the Aesthetic interior: Moorish motifs over the doors, Japanese wallpaper, Eastlake-inspired furniture, peacock feathers...."

Wright's achievements in the medium of art glass are among the most brilliant of his career in decorative design. Working closely with skillful Chicago craftsmen like those of the Linden Glass Company, he realized the ideal that he would describe in a 1928 article for *The Architectural Record*: "Shimmering fabrics—woven of rich glass—patterned in color or stamped to form the metal tracery that is to hold all together to be, in itself, a thing of delicate beauty."

Instead of the traditional lead caming (metal framework), Wright generally specified zinc, sometimes plated with copper, for his architectural glass. In some of his early windows, the design was self-contained; in others, notably the Dana and Robie houses, it was carried across a whole row of windows or doors, or paired to be completed in adjacent panels. As David A. Hanks observes in *The Decorative Designs of Frank Lloyd Wright*: "By changing the windows, Wright changed the rooms—the color, the quality and play of light—each an important consideration. For example, the richly colored 'sumac' windows of the Dana dining room screen most of the light out, contributing to the subdued illumination of the room. The screen of windows, with its conventionalized floral motifs, corresponds to the natural landscape outside."

In the field of art pottery, too, Wright made important contributions, both by his example in preferring Arts and Crafts studio work for his interiors, and by designing such pottery himself. Both Wright and his mentor Louis Sullivan were commissioned to design pieces for the Terra-Cotta and Ceramic Company of Terra Cotta, Illinois (called Teco). As described by David Rago, author of *American Art Pottery* (Saraband, 1997): "Teco ware is typified by soft, medium-green matte finishes that are seldom complicated by layered nuance or secondary glazing....The rectilinear, or geometric, forms...are immediately identifiable by the angular handles and buttresses that adorn the pieces."

It is not surprising that Teco ware became identified as "the pottery of the Prairie School," and many of those influenced by Wright used it in their interiors, including Walter Burley Griffin and George Grant Elmslie. Other American studios that produced work compatible with Wright's organic architecture were Boston's Grueby Pottery and the Pewabic Pottery in Detroit, founded by Mary Chase Perry in 1903.

Wright's adherence to Arts and Crafts principles was not confined to his Prairie house designs, but recurs in new forms throughout his career. It was restated in such diverse materials as plywood and concrete, reprised in the clean, uncluttered lines of his Usonian houses, and carried forward by the many distinguished modern architects who began their careers as members of the Taliesin Fellowship.

Left: A Tiffany-style turtleback lamp of multicolored leaded glass. This style became popular at the turn of the century and is still in demand today.

Below: A bulbous vase glazed in dark colors, made by Grueby Pottery of Boston, Massachusetts, which produced art pottery from 1894 until about 1909. It was perhaps the most influential ceramics studio of its time.

▣ THE ARTS AND CRAFTS AESTHETIC

Frank Lloyd Wright Home & Studio (1889-1909), Oak Park, Ill.

Opposite and above: Familiar Arts and Crafts features of the playroom, opposite, and the stairwell of the Wright home, above, include art-glass doors and windows, spindled screening and frieze above the stairwell, and the decorative mural in the playroom by Orlando Giannini.

Overleaf: Both the Wright studio office (page 52) and the dining room, which was added to the house as the family grew, feature recessed overhead lighting in an ornamental grid and clerestory windows. Built-in shelving houses simple arrangements of native wildflowers in metal containers.

回 EARLY DESIGN SIGNATURES

E.R. Hills-DeCaro House (1906, restored 1976-77), Oak Park, Ill.

Opposite and above: The Hills-DeCaro dining room (opposite) has a built-in mirrored sideboard with wooden piers and simple leaded-glass doors; at the stairwell landing (above), the bay frames a view of the grounds, and heating outlets are concealed.

◙ BRINGING DOWN THE CEILING
William H. Copeland House (1909), Oak Park, Ill.
Left and opposite: Another extensive remodeling was that of the Copeland house, where Wright used an unusual number of wooden bands to lower the eleven-foot height of the original ceilings. Ground-floor rooms were opened up to permit a freer flow of space.

◙ VERTICAL CONTRAST
Harry S. Adams House (1913), Oak Park, Ill.
Right: This wooden door inset with both colored and clear glass adds a vertical note to the long hall that connects dining and living rooms in this two-story brick Prairie house — Wright's last work in Oak Park.

🔲 A DESIGN LANDMARK
William E. Martin House (1903), Oak Park, Ill.

Opposite and above: The Martin house living room, opposite, has notable Arts and Crafts elements, including the built-in bench with shelving above and the large brick fireplace with mantel adorned by simple art pottery. The barrel chair at right was originally designed for the house of this client's brother, Darwin D. Martin of Buffalo, New York. The exterior shows the influence of Secessionist designer Josef Olbrich, a Viennese pioneer of the modern movement. As Hiesinger and Marcus point out in *Landmarks of Twentieth-Century Design* (Abbeville Press, 1993): "There were parallels between the work of the Secession designers and Frank Lloyd Wright, who shared their penchant for rectilinearity and calculated simplicity."

Overleaf: The dining room (page 60) and hall of the William E. Martin house have multiplane bay windows and recessed ceiling lights, respectively. All of the oak furniture was designed by Wright. Note how the Arts and Crafts vases filled with goldenrod complement the interior and reprise the mural above the hall cabinet.

▣ AUTUMNAL COLORS EMBODIED IN GLASS

Frederick C. Robie House (1906), Chicago, Ill.

These pages: The amber and gold colors of the art-glass doors and windows for this house allowed for a constant play of light and shadow. The large bays at either end of the long living/dining area (detail opposite and below) show the recurring geometric forms of the leading, which interacted with other design elements in complex ways. The spherical lighting fixtures shown at right are of the familiar circle-in-a-square type that Wright used extensively at this time.

回 ARTS AND CRAFTS, WEST COAST

John Storer House (1923), Hollywood; Ennis-Brown House (1923), L.A.

Left: The handsome textile-block Storer house has a two-story living room on the top (main) floor that opens to a panoramic view of metropolitan Los Angeles. The 1980s restoration undertaken by Joel Silver in collaboration with Eric Wright restored the house to its original splendor, in keeping with Arts and Crafts principles. The present owner has refurnished it with Wright-designed pieces like the armchairs that flank the fireplace, along with art pottery, textiles and lamps from his outstanding collection. *Below:* Ennis-Brown house living area, detail (see overleaf, page 67).

▣ THE ART-GLASS SPECTRUM

George W. Furbeck House (1897), Oak Park, Il!.
Ennis-Brown House (1923), Los Angeles, Calif.

Opposite and above: Almost thirty years separate the early art-glass examples of the Furbeck house, opposite, from Wright's last use of this feature, in the large-scale California textile-block house designed for Charles Ennis in 1923 (above). This view of the two-story living/dining area shows the clerestory windows, with a wisteria motif, at upper right. The Judson Studios, Los Angeles, produced the glass work. After the house was restored by Mr. and Mrs. August Brown (from 1968), it was turned over to the Trust for Preservation of Cultural Heritage, and its name was changed to the Ennis-Brown House to honor their contribution.

◙ PRAIRIE HOUSE LIGHTING DETAILS
Oak Park and Springfield, Illinois
Above: Hanging lamps from the Peter A. Beachy House;
Left: Copper ceiling grille from the Harry S. Adams House;
Opposite: Fanlight at entrance to the Dana-Thomas House, Springfield, Ill.

THE RICHES, THE MATERIALS

COLOR AND TEXTURE

s we have seen, Wright chose to design every aspect of his interiors, and it is safe to say that his pre-eminent residential designs are those in which he was given a free hand—and, in many cases, a generous budget. His creativity sometimes outstripped his client's resources, and cost overruns were not uncommon. Comfort, too, was sometimes sacrificed to style, as in the case of the familiar high-backed dining chairs, which were often accused of being impossible to sit on. Even Wright complained about them! However, most of his clients were more than satisfied. The Frank Lloyd Wright Archives are filled with testimonials to the power of his work from clients who worked closely with him to achieve results that were beyond their hopes.

The key to the color of many design schemes can be found in the renderings and colored elevations made for client presentations. Designed to be easily read, these drawings came to life in a variety of media: colored pencil and art paper, watercolor, India ink and gouache. Wright's superb draftsmanship is apparent not only in the overall plans, but in such details as flowers, foliage, subtle shading and intricate geometric motifs. Other gifted draftsmen made valuable

Above: *The dining room of the Hills-DeCaro house in Oak Park.*

Page 70: *The dining room of the Meyer May house in Grand Rapids, Michigan (1908), with built-in lighting standards at the corners of the table.*

contributions to these drawings, but Wright's unerring eye and hand are unmistakable. He also painted several notable landscapes in the vicinity of Lake Michigan, now part of the John Lloyd Wright Collection at Columbia University's Avery Library.

Wright's use of color and texture are grounded in the nature of his materials, from structural brick and wood to the linens, silks and woolens used to create his textile designs. From the beginning, he worked with skillful craftspeople like Dorothy Liebes, who studied applied design at the University of California in the early 1920s and learned to weave at Chicago's Hull House. Ten years after Liebes opened her San Francisco studio in 1930, *House and Garden* magazine called her "America's acknowledged leader in the field of hand-loomed fabrics."

Henning Watterston, another notable weaver, visited Taliesin in 1941 and made the curtain Wright had designed for the Hillside Theater—a colorful abstraction of Taliesin itself. When this curtain was destroyed by fire during the 1950s, the women at Taliesin made a replacement of colored felt and yarn appliquéd on fabric. It was given to Wright for his birthday as a surprise.

Another fixture at Taliesin for some years was the rug originally designed for the Maximilian Hoffman house in Rye, New York (1955). It has bold geometric patterns in shades of rust, red, green, blue and gold. Other fabrics specified for the Hoffman house were designed by Jack Lenor Larsen, including a 90-percent silk weave called Old Gold, which had lurex threads that reflected the sparkling mica chips in the stonework.

The striking rug designed for the David Wright house in Phoenix (1950), with exu-

Below: Art-glass window and leaded ceiling lights at the Meyer May house: the window detailing is copper-sheathed.

berant arcs and circles that repeat the circular grid of the house, was produced to Wright's design by V'Soske carpetmakers. Another example from his postwar career is the Albert Adelman house rug, woven for a Usonian residence in Fox Point, Arizona (1948). Its subtle shades of olive, red, orange and blue on a gold ground harmonize with the buff-colored concrete block construction material.

Unfortunately, few of the rugs designed during and after the Prairie house era have survived. Some outstanding examples from the period incude the elegant runners made for the Heurtley house in Oak Park (1902), which had an arrow pattern offset by geometric forms; and the 1916 rug for Milwaukee's Bogk house, with a geometric cross-shaped design that repeated the square detailing of the furniture. For Tokyo's Imperial Hotel (1915–22), Wright designed hundreds of yards of carpeting and rugs that were custom woven in China. It is not surprising that this eight-year project involved more than 700 drawings: it encompassed furniture, sculpture, murals, glass, tableware, linens and upholstery fabrics. Fortunately, some of these designs have been restored to production under the auspices of the Frank Lloyd Wright Foundation. Tiffany & Co., for example, is marketing both the "Imperial" white-and-gold china designed for the hotel's formal dining room and colorful examples of the informal "Cabaret" china used in its supper club.

Architect and historian Thomas A. Heinz, some of whose photographs appear in this book, provides a wealth of information about the furniture and fittings designed for Wright rooms. In describing the Avery Coonley Prairie house — second only to the Robie house — in Riverside, Illinois (1907), he calls attention to the prairie fern design carved into the grille that covers the indirect lighting and to the end (or flower) table in the living room: "One of the most refined of all Wright's small tables. The outward flare of the legs gives it a sense of stability. . . . The table within a table of the shelf structure adds to the interest, as does the shelf at the centre." (*Frank Lloyd Wright Interiors and Furniture*).

In the same source, Heinz observes that the unusual wooden floor lamp designed for the Sherman Booth house (1915) in Glencoe, Illinois, was "derived from the Japanese print stands used in the exhibition at the Art Institute of Chicago." In fact, Wright was involved in mounting numerous exhibitions, both of his work and of his notable print collection, from the early 1900s onward. In 1902 his rectilinear "cube chair," which John Lloyd Wright described as "the first piece of modern furniture made in this country," was shown at the Chicago Architectural Club. He often exhibited at the Art Institute of Chicago, and helped to install his exhibitions at the Art Club of Chicago as well. In 1953, after the exhibit "Sixty Years of Living Architecture" had toured Europe, it came to New York City, where it was housed in Wright's Usonian Exhibition House, now the site of the Guggenheim Museum. Undoubtedly, these experiences contributed to his mastery of decorative design in the realms of art and architecture.

Anne Massey, in *Interior Design of the 20th Century* (Thames and Hudson, World of Art Series), speaks to Wright's influence on the European movement De Stijl (the Style), founded in Holland in 1917. Its leaders were familiar with Wright's work through its German publication, the *Wasmuth Portfolio*. The group included the painter Piet Mondrian, designer Gerrit Rietveld and theorist Theo van Doesburg, who also painted and designed. The new aesthetic was summed up in van Doesburg's 1924 article "Sixteen Points of a Plastic Architecture," in which he stated that "the new architecture is *anti-cubic*, that is to say, it does not try to freeze the different functional space-cells into one closed cube. Rather it throws the functional space cells (as well as overhanging planes, balcony, volumes etc.) centrifugally from the core." This is an accurate description of the "pinwheel plan" Prairie houses originated by Wright. Massey also states that "Rietveld was inspired by Japanese house design, and by the work of Frank Lloyd Wright." It is not surprising that Wright's view of color and texture as integral to design, and his gift for draftsmanship, would influence so many twentieth-century artists and designers.

On the domestic scene, Wright's designs were instrumental in undermining architectural features he deplored — attics, basements, double-hung sash windows (he called them "guillotines") and visible heating elements like radiators ("eye-sores" and "abominations"). Wright would go to any lengths to disguise a radiator, including windowseats, bookcases, built-in piers and rectilinear covers. Wherever possible, he used forced-air heating, and in the Usonian houses he got rid of the radiator entirely by embedding the heating elements in the concrete floors.

Given the comfort and beauty of Wright's interior designs throughout his seventy-five-year career, it is no wonder that his work is becoming even more widely known and appreciated than it was during his lifetime. By combining the best of the past with the potential inherent in modern technology, he achieved a unique synthesis that retains its power as a new century dawns.

Opposite: *The Edgar J. Kaufmann, Sr., house, called Fallingwater, designed during the 1930s, when Wright's career began anew and flourished for another twenty-five years.*

▣ STYLE CHANGES

Aline Barnsdall House (1917), Los Angeles Calif.
William G. Fricke House (1901), Oak Park, Ill.

Opposite and above: Wright struck a new design note in his furniture for the Hollyhock (Barnsdall) House dining room in Los Angeles, opposite. The tall chair backs have the stylized hollyhock motif on rectangular planes that resemble a trellis. This abstraction recurs on the base of the hexagonal table and on the room's richly paneled walls. In the 1901 Fricke dining room, the ensemble has lower-backed chairs with a single slat between top rail and seat. Architect Webster Tomlinson collaborated on the design of the Fricke house.

▣ DRAMATIC NEW HEIGHTS
Dana-Thomas House (1902), Springfield, Ill.

These pages: The two-story dining room with barrel vault on the opposite page has a George Niedecken mural of prairie plants that continues the autumnal color scheme used throughout this expensive thirty-five-room house. At right, a detail of the geometric art glass produced for the Susan Lawrence Dana mansion by the Linden Glass Company of Chicago. The exterior of this imposing house, below, with its pagoda-like roofline, soon made it a Springfield landmark. It has been owned by the State of Illinois since 1981.

◙ "SHIMMERING FABRICS" OF GLASS
Dana-Thomas House (1902), Springfield, Ill.

These pages: The prairie sumac motif, abstracted in complex chevrons of clear and colored glass, is reprised in some 450 pieces of art glass commissioned for this house—an unprecedented achievement in modern decorative design. Windows, doors, skylights, fanlights—all contribute to the rich ambience of a stately home that served as an art gallery and salon for its original owner.

▣ TOTAL DESIGN

The Meyer May House (1908), Grand Rapids, Mich.
Left and above: This serene exemplar of the Prairie house style shows Wright's hand in every aspect of the design. The windows repeat the squares and stylized leaf forms that are incorporated into the carpeting, lighting fixtures, embroidered linens and other elements of the composition. The prevailing tones are green and gold. A Tiffany-style turtleback lamp sheds a warm glow on the view of the snow-covered garden and terraces framed by the window. The exterior view above shows the wide, shallow planters whose cascades of foliage and flowers soften the horizontal planes of the outdoor living space through the summer months.

回 HARMONIOUS COLOR AND TEXTURE

Dana-Thomas House (1902), Springfield, Ill.
Robert L. Wright House (1953), Bethesda, Maryland

Opposite: The plaster wall panels of the two-story entry hall of the Dana-Thomas house were heavily trowelled to produce a rough surface that contrasts with the smooth areas of brick, wood and glass. As architectural historian Thomas A. Heinz points out in *Frank Lloyd Wright Interiors and Furniture* (Academy Group Ltd, 1994), the effect is "quite lively when powders of different colors are mixed into the final coat. When examined closely, it resembles a painting by Monet or Seurat because of the small areas of rich color." This masonry detailing was done throughout the house.

Below: Designed for the architect's son Robert L. Wright, the Usonian Robert L. Wright house is a solar hemicycle of concrete and Philippine mahogany with a polished concrete floor. Wright duplicated the shape of the house in the low table with hassocks seen in the foreground. The subtle range of colors, like the informal furniture and fittings, are in keeping with the simplicity of the Usonian house aesthetic.

◨ A CONTEMPORARY CLASSIC

The Donald Schaberg House (1950), Okemos, Mich.
Opposite and above: Two views of the continuous, restful
living space in this Usonian house show the interplay of
strong simple planes of brick, wood and glazing. Deep
tones of red, blue and brown in furniture and fittings complement the construction materials. Note the slat-back
barrel chairs, an evolution of the design first used in the
Darwin D. Martin house almost fifty years before.

Overleaf: A panoramic view of the central kitchen and
dining area, with burnished earth-tone pottery and plantings, which overlooks a broad wooded valley. The concept
of a "living kitchen" area was a Usonian innovation made
to reflect the disappearance of domestic servants and the
growing informality of contemporary American life.

COMFORT AT MODERATE COST

Goetsch-Winkler House (1939), Okemos, Mich.
Lowell Walter House (1945), Quasqueton, Iowa

Opposite and above: The area conducive to quiet reading
and study on the opposite page is part of the moderately
priced Usonian house built for two teachers at what is
now Michigan State University: Alma Goetsch and
Katherine Winkler. Redwood board-and-batten forms the
backdrop for the colorful geometric rug, and a bronze-
based table lamp with art-glass shade provides subdued
lighting. The postwar Walter house, above, makes effective
and economical use of concrete, steel, walnut and brick.

⊡ "WINDOW WALLS" TO A PRIVATE GARDEN

The Donald Schaberg House (1950), Okemos, Mich.
Above: This daytime view of the Schaberg dining area shows that the interior space is continuous with the terraced courtyard, with its brick walls and cedar-shake roofing. Most of the Usonian houses faced inward, emphasizing privacy, rather than outward, toward the street side.

⊡ RARE PRESENCE AND PROPORTIONS

William Palmer House (1950), Ann Arbor, Mich.
Opposite and overleaf: This richly appointed Usonian house, whose triangular plan is incised into the polished flooring, melds the warm tones of cypress and sand-mold brick to create an interior of unusual depth and beauty. Red and gold predominate throughout the living area, enhanced by the metal ornamentation of the brick pier beside the grand piano (overleaf).

▣ A USONIAN LANDMARK
Melvyn Maxwell Smith House (1946), Bloomfield Hills, Mich.

Opposite and above: This postwar Usonian combines the jewel tones of the built-in seating with the tawny colors of brick and cypress. The geometric planes of the furniture and shelving contrast with the jagged pattern of the recessed lighting grids above the dining room table. The L-shaped plan of the house is apparent in the view of the living area (above), where the rounded forms of decorative objects set off the rectilinear fireplace and window-wall.

◙ WARMTH AND SOLIDITY

Arthur Heurtley House (1902), Oak Park, Ill.

Right: This handsome living room from one of the first Prairie houses, only a block from Wright's home studio, shows why the Heurtley house remained one of the architect's favorites. The fireplace of Roman brick has a double arch reminiscent of Henry Hobson Richardson's work, while the dramatic molding, recessed ceiling lights and casement windows are Wright design signatures.

AT WORK IN STONE

right's use of durable stone, and masonry materials including brick, terra-cotta (oven-baked clay), concrete block and poured concrete, made him part of a line that extended back some 6,000 years. Kiln-burned brick can still be found on the site of the vanished city of Babylon, although most of it has disintegrated into its constituent clay. The ancient Egyptians used clay from the Nile riverbed, often mixed with a straw binder, to make building bricks and tiles. Both the Greeks and the Romans used masonry to construct their homes and monuments, and the Romans were especially adept at tile manufacture. They used fired clay pipe to carry water and sewage, and made decorative reliefs of terra-cotta to adorn their buildings.

Wright's early experiments in the use of masonry had their influence on the young European architects who followed his work in such magazines as *The Studio* and the Parisian *Revue Blanche*. Like him, they sought building materials suitable to contemporary needs. They used steel, glass and reinforced concrete as structural elements, which did away with the need for massive masonry bases and load-bearing walls. New steel and concrete "armatures" allowed for glazed

Above: *The postwar
Howard Anthony house
(1949), built of stone
and cypress on a wooded
site overlooking the St.
Joseph River in Benton
Harbor, Michigan.*

Page 100: *The two-story
drafting room in Wright's
Oak Park studio, with a
rough-hewn brick fireplace
flanked by brick tiers and
surmounted by a frieze.*

walls, doors and bands of windows without compromising the strength or structural
viability of the building. Modern architecture began to move, as Wright put it, "out
of the ground and into the light."

When Wright began his career, it was still common practice to have bricks molded on
the site from nearby clay deposits. Today, they are generally made by huge machines
that can produce up to 300,000 wire-cut bricks per day. But regardless of the technology used, the basic processes remain the same: the mixture of clay with other substances
like sand, as needed; formation and drying of the new bricks; and kiln-firing, followed
by a cooling period. Brick color depends on the composition of the clay used—high
proportions of iron produce bricks of red, buff or salmon, while the presence of chalk
yields bricks of a sulfur-yellow color.

For much of his career, Wright favored the use of narrow Roman brick, which laid
up into smoothly surfaced walls whose texture and pattern could be varied in several
ways. The mortar used to join the bricks could be tooled into various shapes, raked
deeply, or cut flush. Sometimes Wright added gold-colored particles to the mortar for a
rich, subtle effect, or had the bricks set in courses that were alternately recessed and
projecting, as seen in the plates that follow.

When building in stone, he used native stone quarried nearby wherever possible. This
was the case at his Wisconsin home/studio, Taliesin, which was built and rebuilt several
times. The light-colored local limestone was shaped into walls and piers in rough, alternating courses that resembled the natural rock formations. At Fallingwater, he used local

sandstone to the same effect, and harmonized its buff color with chamois-colored concrete cantilevers that carried the house above the stream and its wooded ravine. Sometimes his experiments were not successful: when he specified that decomposed local granite be mixed with the concrete for the massive Ennis-Brown house because of its color value, the granite had an adverse effect on durability. Years later, large sections of the retaining wall collapsed. However, Wright could (sometimes) admit his mistakes, and he reflected later that he had exceeded the limits of his material in this house: "[It] was way out of concrete-block size. I think that was carrying it too far."

Given the sculptural quality of his work, it is not surprising that Wright often collaborated with sculptors, notably Richard Bock and Orlando Giannini. Bock made the sculptured capitals for the entryway to Wright's Oak Park studio. He also created a terra-cotta relief for the innovative brick Larkin Building in Buffalo (demolished 1949) and a sculptural frieze for Chicago's Isidore Heller house (1896). One of his best-known works is *The Flower in the Crannied Wall*, at the entrance to the Dana-Thomas house in Springfield, Illinois. Designed in collaboration with Wright, this naturalistic female figure represents the architect as artist, holding a building that is still in the process of creation. Bock also designed the fountain in the two-story foyer of the Dana-Thomas house.

Orlando Giannini was both a sculptor and a painter. During the 1880s, he managed the Cincinnati Art Pottery group and later executed several murals for the Wright house remodeling in Oak Park (1895). He also worked in art glass, including glass mosaics for wall panels and mantel facings. Unfortunately, some of the best examples, including the mantel facing for the Darwin D. Martin house in Buffalo, have disappeared.

Both Bock and Giannini worked closely with Wright on the lavish Chicago entertainment complex called Midway Gardens (1913). Sponsored by Edward C. Waller, Jr., it was modeled on the great beer gardens of Germany and included a year-round restaurant called the Winter Garden and a series of terraces with a large outdoor bandshell,

Left: *The Aline Barnsdall Hollyhock House (1917), with its exposed poured-concrete masonry, has affinities with Wright's Unity Temple of 1904 in Oak Park.*

Above: *Bold redwood diagonals emphasize the rugged rubblestone base and triangular piers at Taliesin West (1937) in Scottsdale, Arizona.*

the Summer Garden. The block-square project was built of richly patterned concrete block and brick. With Iannelli, Wright designed a series of playful abstract figures he called sprites to ornament the complex. A few of these remain in private collections, but most were destroyed when the Gardens were razed in 1929. Bock's contribution included a large relief cast in concrete for the walls of the inside stairway.

Another successful experiment in masonry was Wright's winter home/studio at Scottsdale, Arizona, begun in 1937. Built entirely by members of the Taliesin Fellowship, it has massive base walls and chimneys of desert rubblestone embedded in concrete. Most of the desert rocks used to build the complex had one flat side, which was left exposed when the concrete was poured into the forms. Then the surplus mortar was chipped away from the edges; sometimes the stone was washed with acid to bring out its colors, ranging from mauve to reddish-brown. The result is a series of rugged buildings, linked by broad, shallow steps, terraces and covered walkways, that rises like a natural formation from the desert around it.

Another essay in desert rubblestone was the Rose Pauson house (1939) in Phoenix, which was devastated by fire in 1942. According to Carla Lind, the author of *Lost Wright*, this dramatic Usonian house had "walls of lapped wood over canted, dark red stone and concrete....Inside, the house was constructed as if it were a fine piece of furniture, each board custom milled six times before being carefully finished. The two-story living room had twelve-foot-high windows opening to outdoor terraces that served to double the living space."

Some of Wright's last works show the increasing plasticity in his use of concrete that marked the postwar years. The most obvious example is New York City's Guggenheim Museum, first envisioned in 1943, but unbuilt until the late 1950s. Its expanding-spiral form was achieved by the use of both sprayed and poured concrete.

A curvilinear concrete design was also used for the house designed in Phoenix for the architect's son, David Wright, in 1952. As Mary Hollingsworth describes it in *Architecture of the 20th Century*: "The David Wright house is built on thick, trunklike stilts, with a circle of rooms grouped around a central space. Unlike the Guggenheim, this central space is closed off from the house for practical reasons, but the Guggenheim helix features in the gently spiraling ramp, through which the building is reached, and the furniture Wright designed for the house echoes its circular form." Whimsically, Wright called the building "David's treehouse," because it rose above the landscape around it.

Throughout his career, Wright showed himself a master of masonry, employing it in innovative and beautiful ways to create lasting works of commercial, ecclesiastical and residential architecture. His achievements in these labor-intensive materials are among his greatest contributions to modern architecture and decorative design.

Left: *The Mayan silhouette of the John Storer house (1923) was created by plain, pierced and patterned concrete blocks laid up in alternating courses and joined by steel rods.*

EARLY ESSAYS IN BRICKWORK
George Furbeck House (1897), Oak Park, Ill.

Opposite and above: Two distinctive brick fireplaces are the focal points of the Furbeck dining room (opposite) and living room (above). In the dining room, the recessed hearth of Roman brick is surmounted by narrow panels of alternating brick and glass and framed in oak molding. The octagonal living room has a wide brick fireplace with courses projecting in bands at regular intervals to emphasize the horizontal line.

▣ USONIAN HOUSE MASONRY

The Eric V. Brown House (1949), Kalamazoo, Mich.

Above and opposite: Masonry walls and a complementing central fireplace contrast with warm wood detailing and ceilings in the Eric V. Brown House, which combined unpatterned concrete blocks and mahogany. The uphill roofline ascends from ground level. Built-in shelving accommodated the Browns' art collection, which was displayed to advantage against the neutral-colored masonry. A full view of the rugged concrete-and-brick fireplace, above, shows the hearth defined by irregular standing stones. This house was one of four designed for Kalamazoo's Parkwyn Village project.

▣ COLORS OF THE DESERT

Taliesin West (1937), Scottsdale, Ariz.

Overleaf: The massive masonry of this Wright home/studio is of desert rubblestone and concrete. The warm tones of the rough stone, each piece unique in shape and hue, are enhanced by the natural light and accented with smoothly polished wood furnishings. The geometric shapes of the furniture, windows and moldings provide a contrast with the irregular rubblestones.

◙ A STUDY IN CONTRASTS

**Howard Anthony House (1949),
Benton Harbor, Mich.
Aline Barnsdall House (1917), Los Angeles, Calif.**

Above and opposite: More than thirty years separate the Usonian design of the Anthony house, above, from that of the Barnsdall (Hollyhock) house, opposite, in southern California. The Anthony fireplace core ascends jaggedly to a triangular juncture with the cypress ceiling. The irregular stonework in this diamond-shaped house is mirrored by the exterior.

At Hollyhock House, geometric motifs in concrete relief surmount the massive fireplace, which contributes to the Mayan feeling of the structure. With the skylit reflecting pool in front of the hearth, Wright symbolically combined the elements of fire and water.

◙ ORNAMENTAL BRICK INTERIORS

Donald Schaberg House (1950), Okemos, Mich.
Robie House (1906), Chicago, Ill.

Above and opposite: According to Wright historian William A. Storrer, 55,000 bricks were used to construct the single-story Donald Schaberg house, above. This Usonian house originally had an L-shaped plan. Seen here is a view of the brick and glazed walls adjacent to the courtyard. The low, triangular brick projection houses a pool and fountain.

A close view of the Roman-brick fireplace "screen" that defines the long Robie house living/dining area, opposite, shows an earlier ornamental brick feature in a Prairie style interior. Note the opening at the center, which provides an unobstructed view of the molded ceiling planes that are continuous between the two areas. What appears to be a single rug is actually one of six diferent pieces custom-woven for the main floor.

▣ GEOMETRIC CONTRASTS
The Herbert F. Johnson House (1937), Wind Point, Wisc.

These pages: Opposite, a view of the three-story rounded brick chimney core, which rises thirty feet through tiers of clerestory windows. The spiral staircase ascends to a rooftop observatory. Smooth, rectangular slab steps lead to the library level, above, which has cushioned tabourets to provide additional seating. Above the masonry wood-box is the mezzanine level, enclosed by curving golden-oak veneer. The south façade, right, shows the brick colonnade overlooking the pool.

▣ PLAIN AND PATTERNED CONCRETE BLOCK

The Ennis-Brown House (1923), Los Angeles, Calif.
Opposite and below: The bold geometric patterns of the Ennis-Brown house blocks are in keeping with both the size and complexity of this monumental residence. Unadorned blocks create a rhythmic interplay with textured material. The view of the two-story entry hall, opposite, focuses upon the gold-toned Tiffany mosaic of wisteria above the fireplace, which is absracted for the art-glass clerestory windows.

◙ "USONIA II"

Herbert Jacobs House (1948), Middleton, Wisc.

Above: This is the second of the Usonian houses, the first of which was also designed for the Jacobs family, in Westmoreland, Wisconsin (1936). Called a solar hemicyle, it has a curved shape and glazed southern exposure, with the back wall, of masonry, set into the earth. The house conforms to Wright's ideal of a moderately priced dwelling for American families, as expressed in his January 1938 article for *The Architectural Forum*: "We must have as big a living room with as much garden coming into it as we can afford, with a fireplace in it, and bookshelves, dining table, benches and living room tables built in."

◙ ABSTRACT FLORAL MOTIFS IN CONCRETE

Samuel Freeman House (1923), Los Angeles, Calif.

Opposite: Floral motifs on pierced and patterned concrete block enrich the two-story living room of the Freeman house, Wright's third essay in textile-block construction. Rudolf Schindler designed the furniture for this house, and Lloyd Wright supervised the project from the Los Angeles office opened by Wright in 1917.

LIVING SYMPATHY WITH NATURE

ORGANIC INSPIRATION

Among the influences on Wright's creation of buildings that are, as he put it, in "living sympathy with nature," one of the most apparent is his feeling for Japanese art and architecture. In his 1917 work The Japanese Print (Horizon Press reprint, 1967), Wright spoke of "that interior harmony which penetrates the outward form or letter and is its determining character; that quality in the thing…that is its significance and its life for us." In the belief that Japanese culture had attained this aesthetic ideal (he called it "poetry"), he looked to the East for insight into that "determining character" of architecture that could be reinterpreted for the needs of a modern democratic society.

Perhaps his first exposure to Japanese architecture outside the realm of art was the half-scale replica of a Fujiwara-period wooden temple reconstructed for the World's Columbian Exposition at Chicago in 1893. It was in stark contrast to most of the other buildings at the fair—a neoclassic montage created by Beaux Arts architects. Even as Wright and Sullivan worked on the Golden Door for the fair's Transportation Building, they saw the exhibition as a major setback for the newly established Chicago School of architecture.

Above: *The harmonious Meyer May house in Grand Rapids, Michigan, was designed in 1908, the same year that Wright published an essay, "In the Cause of Architecture," that described his buildings as "organic abstractions." He explained that they "sympathize with the trees and foliage around them" and "may be said to blossom with the season."*

Page 122: *Patterned cypress paneling and recessed skylights link this secluded corner of the Smith house to the garden in Bloomfield Hills, Michigan.*

But the revival of classical models was short-lived in the face of Chicago's rapid progress into a modern architecture of strong, simple forms that were closer in spirit to the Japanese temple than to the Beaux Arts marble colonnades.

Sullivan would follow the trail blazed by Chicago architect William Le Baron Jenney in the use of steel-frame construction for the modern skyscraper, adding a new dimension of beauty through the principle of organic architecture enunciated by John Ruskin. And Wright's residential designs on the same principle would transform the single-family home into a lived experience rather than a collection of spaces. In his writings, literary and musical metaphors occur repeatedly, as when he states: "Like poetry, the sense of architecture is the sound of the within."

Many architectural historians have commented on the resemblance between Wright's open floor plans and those of the Japanese folkhouse. As early as 1909, C.R. Ashbee of the British Arts and Crafts movement said of the notable California architect Charles Sumner Greene: "Like Lloyd Wright, the spell of Japan is upon him; he feels the beauty and makes magic out of the horizontal line."

The best-known example of Greene's work, carried out with his brother and partner, architect Henry Mather Greene, is the David B. Gamble house in Pasadena (1908), a multilevel bungalow clearly influenced by the Far East. The Gamble interior is a study in design motifs inspired by the Greenes' collection of Japanese prints and books on Oriental art and architecture. Like Wright, the Greenes delighted in the use of fine woods — native redwood, mahogany, ebony — and they, too, favored low, horizontal rooflines and broad eaves that gave protection from the California sun. The Greenes also designed the furniture, lighting fixtures, stained glass and landscaping for their houses. The principal point on which they diverged from Wright was in their insistence on hand craftsmanship as opposed to exploring the artistic potential inherent in skillful machine work.

Obviously, this made their designs available only to the wealthy—an inconsistency that William Morris himself had been unable to resolve.

Meanwhile, young European architects were coming into the United States with their own ideas on modern architecture. What would be called the International Style generates controversy to this day, as seen in Tom Wolfe's entertaining book *From Bauhaus to Our House* (1990). The British architect Peter Davey made his case in 1980, when he stated that "The really international style of the '20s and '30s was not the Modern Movement, as some historians have made out, but classicism in different guises, ranging from the people's palaces of Russia and Germany to the quaint neo-colonial and neo-Georgian of Anglo-Saxon suburbs. It was not until after the second world war that the Modern Movement was victorious" (*Architecture of the Arts and Crafts Movement*, Rizzoli).

Davey faults the influential German architect Walter Gropius, founder of the Bauhaus, for moving away from his original emphasis on craftsmanship to espouse the machine-age collaboration of artist and industrialist. He states that "Gropius was in fact wedded to machines," and adds: "Over the next fifty years, standardization, machine worship and distrust of the craftsman gradually became some of the dominating themes of architecture."

Other architects, including Edgar Kaufmann, Jr., who studied with Wright, took a very different view of the Modern movement. Kaufmann was the curator of the Museum of Modern Art's 1947 exhibition "Modern Rooms of the Last Fifty Years." This was the point of departure for his 1953 book *What Is Modern Interior Design?*, in which, according to Anne Massey, "[he] traced the evolution of the Modern interior from William Morris via the Bauhaus, culminating with Frank Lloyd Wright." The book was published only six years before Wright died—still hard at work, although many of his last projects were never executed.

Below: The eminently livable Usonian house designed for the Smiths in 1946 was enlarged in 1969–70 by Taliesin Associated Architects to meet the owners' needs. Growing as it goes, the house is a seamless garment of brick and cypress sheltered by maturing trees.

Wright's postwar designs increasingly reflected his visionary "city of broad acres," as seen in the unbuilt projects for the soaring Point View Residence in Pittsburgh, Pennsylvania, and the Garden of Eden complex for Baghdad, Iraq. They bore no resemblance to the prevailing International Style. In fact, that ambiguous term had been coined by young American architects and critics to describe the Europeans they admired most, including Le Corbusier, Gropius and Mies van der Rohe. As Mary Hollingsworth points out in *Architecture of the 20th Century*, "In deliberately rejecting the authoritarianism of the International Style, Wright set himself apart from the mainstream of architectural design after World War II."

Perhaps the house that best illustrates Wright's evolution as an organic architect is Taliesin, which was, in effect, a work in progress from 1911 until his death in 1959. In fact, Wright's last sketch was for the garden he designed there for his wife, which was planted that summer. Taliesin follows the contours of its site above the Wisconsin River—"of the hill, not on the hill," as Wright described it. Built mainly of native limestone, timber and plaster surfacing, its terraces and balconies reach out to unite the house and its walled gardens with the larger landscape beyond, a feature of Oriental art and architecture.

One of the world's best-known private residences, Taliesin has maintained its sense of repose and self-containment through decades of habitation, cultivation and expansion. It is an exemplar of Wright's life and work, which he summed up in a moving statement made shortly before his death: "All the more because I study Nature do I revere God, because Nature is all the body of God we will ever know."

Opposite: At the John Storer house (1923), a California classic, luxuriant tropical plantings both conceal and reveal the entryway, softening the blocky lines of the structure much as jungle growth obscures the monolithic forms of pre-Columbian Mayan temples.

Below: The Goetsch-Winkler House (1939) in its naturally wooded Michigan setting. During the summer, a wildflower garden and built-in window boxes enhance the view from the vertical windows.

◉ A USONIAN HAVEN

Goetsch-Winkler House (1939), Okemos, Mich.

The Midwestern Usonian built for Alma Goetsch and Katherine Winkler in 1939 has triple-tiered cantilevered eaves and inexpensive, durable materials for low maintenance and a high degree of comfort and privacy. The welcoming open-plan living space features a brick chimney core and built-in seating and bookcases, and is lighted by clerestory windows of clear glass.

▣ RESTFUL WITHIN AND WITHOUT
Donald Schaberg House (1950), Okemos, Mich.

Opposite and above: A bedroom in warm earth tones of wood and brick, with a corner window of mitred glass that does not obstruct the view, provides a light, peaceful space within which to enjoy the woodland setting. Note the Wright-designed table lamp, which was also in use at Taliesin. The exterior view above shows how the sense of shelter is enhanced by the broad eaves, whose light-colored soffits (undersides) provide continuity with the cream-colored ceilings inside. By day, they reflect more light into the rooms.

回 NATURAL TREASURES

These pages: As John Lloyd Wright recalled in his biography of his famous parent, "Father liked weeds." It is easy to see why, when we find these common field and roadside plants used to such good effect: in the Dana-Thomas house (opposite), Wright's Oak Park office (above) and the foyer of the William E Martin house. These informal arrangements are entirely at home with both the Japanese prints displayed in Wright's office and the stylized mural above the Martin sideboard.

◙ REMODELING FOR A NEW CENTURY
Peter A. Beachy House (1906), Oak Park, Ill.

Right: It is hard to believe that this contemporary interior evolved from a 19th-century Gothic cottage, which Wright remodeled completely. The dining area shows how oak molding was used with a wide plaster band at ceiling level to lower the height of the original room to human scale. All of the cherry-wood furniture is original to the house. Note the decorative beam that supports the lighting fixtures, which resembles a Shinto *torii*, or temple gate.

▣ GENIUS AT WORK

The Edgar J. Kaufmann, Sr., House
"Fallingwater" (1935), Mill Run, Penn.

Left: This uniquely beautiful country house, with natural boulders in the rock ledge below incorporated into the hearth, was the Kaufmann family's retreat for some twenty-five years. Mrs. Kaufmann added the antique chairs at the dining table and other personal touches. The floor is of waxed flagstone, and Cherokee-red accents brighten the huge living area, in which natural buffs and greys predominate.

回 TALIESIN: HOME, SCHOOL AND STUDIO
Taliesin (1911–1959), Spring Green, Wisc.

These pages: With the foundation of the Taliesin Fellowship in 1932, Wright's rural home/studio grew steadily to encompass the former Hillside Home School (Playhouse, opposite) and larger living quarters in the main house to accommodate visitors. The vibrant colors used in the theatre mark it as what Wright called "a good time place," while the living quarters show the Usonian transition to lighter, unstained oak and plywood furniture like the "origami" chairs and hexagonal table.

▣ A LINEAR SYNTAX

Gregor Affleck House (1940), Bloomfield Hills, Mich.
Frederick C. Robie House (1906), Chicago, Ill.

Opposite and above: Much as Chicago's Robie House (above) exemplifies the Prairie style, the Affleck residence represents the angles and planes of Wright's model for Broadacre City. Identified on the model as "a home for sloping ground," its sun room and sleeping quarters are at ground level, with cantilevered living space and balcony above. Brick and cypress are the primary construction materials. Wright's mid-century vision of "the Disappearing City" sprang from the same roots as his earliest work—the pure abstraction of natural forms.

GLOSSARY

The following brief definitions cover architectural and interior design terms used in this book.

baluster: A row of miniature columns or spindles supporting a stair rail, or arranged to form decorative screens etc.

batten: A narrow strip of wood used between boards, as for flooring or siding, to prevent warping

breakfront: A sideboard or cabinet with a projecting central section

buttress: Masonry pier used for reinforcement of walls

caming: Metal framework for an art-glass window or panel, usually made of lead; also called "leading"

cantilever: A projecting beam or other structure supported at only one end

capital: The top part, or head, of a pillar or column

casement window: A narrow window with sashes that open outward on hinges

clerestory: A series of windows at or near ceiling height, or rising into a separate story

colonnade: A row of columns connected at the top in the classical manner

coping: The top layer of a masonry wall

elevation: A flat scale drawing of the front, rear, or side of a building

fanlight: A half-circle window, often with sash bars arranged like the ribs of a fan

frame: The supporting structure, or skeleton, of a building

fretwork: Ornamental three-dimensional geometric designs or other symmetrical figures (frets) enclosed in a band or border

frieze: Decorative band around a wall

hassock: A thick cushion used as a footstool

hip: The angle formed by the meeting of two adjacent sloping sides of a roof

inlaid: Decorated with veneers of fine materials set into the surface

load-bearing: Capable of carrying a load in addition to its own weight

mullion: Vertical window division

pedestal urn: A wide, shallow urn on a footed base, often used as a planter

pier: Supporting post or stone, often square, thicker than a column

portico: Colonnaded entry porch

settee: A seat for two or more people with a back and, in most cases, arms

settle: A long wooden seat or bench with arms and a high back

siding: Boards, shingles, or other material used to surface a frame building

soffit: The underside of a structural component—eaves, beams, arches etc.

stringcourses: Wooden moldings used to define sections of a wall or ceiling

stucco: A durable finish for exterior walls, applied wet and usually composed of cement, sand and lime

tabouret: A low stool that resembles a table

terra cotta: A hard, semifired ceramic clay used in pottery and building construction

vault: Arched roof or ceiling

veneer: A very thin layer of wood or other material for facing or inlaying wood. Also, thin layers of wood glued together to form plywood for building purposes

ACKNOWLEDGEMENTS

The publisher would like to thank the owners of each of the houses featured in this book for generously allowing the photographers access to their homes; as well as the following individuals for their assistance in the preparation of this book: Charles J. Ziga, art director; Wendy J. Ciaccia, graphic designer; Nicola Gillies, editorial assistant; Lisa Langone Desautels, indexer. All photographs are © Balthazar Korab or © Christian Korab except those on pages: 34–5, 85, 91, 98–9, 120, 121 (Photographs by Thomas A. Heinz, © 1998 Copyright Thomas A. Heinz); 47t, 48, 49 (© David Rago); 47b (courtesy of the William Morris Gallery, Walthamstow, London). All photographs of the Dana-Thomas House are reproduced by courtesy of the Illinois Historic Preservation Agency.

BIBLIOGRAPHY

Anscombe, Isabelle. *Arts & Crafts Style*. London: Phaidon Press, 1991.

Carver, Norman F., Jr. *Japanese Folkhouses*. Kalamazoo, Mich.:Documan Press, 1984.

Crawford, Alan. *Charles Rennie Mackintosh*, World of Art series. London: Thames and Hudson, 1995.

Davey, Peter. *Architecture of the Arts and Crafts Movement*. N.Y.: Rizzoli, 1980.

Guerrero, Pedro E. *Picturing Wright: An Album from Frank Lloyd Wright's Photographer*. S.F.: Pomegranate Artbooks, 1994.

Hanks, David A. *The Decorative Designs of Frank Lloyd Wright*. N.Y.: E.P. Dutton, 1979.

Heinz, Thomas A. *Frank Lloyd Wright Interiors and Furniture*. London: Academy Group Ltd., 1994.

_____. *Frank Lloyd Wright Field Guide, vol l, Upper Great Lakes: Minn., Wisc., Mich*. London: Academy Group, Ltd, 1996.

Hiesinger, Kathryn B., and George H. Marcus. *Landmarks of Twentieth-Century Design: An Illustrated Handbook*. N.Y.: Abbeville Press, 1993.

Hoffmann, Donald. *Frank Lloyd Wright's Fallingwater: The House and Its History*, 2nd rev. ed. Mineola, N.Y.: Dover Pubns., 1993.

Hollingsworth, Mary. *Architecture of the 20th Century*. London: Brompton Books, 1988.

Larson, George A., and Jay Pridmore. *Chicago Architecture and Design*. N.Y.: Harry N. Abrams, 1993.

Lind, Carla. *Lost Wright: Frank Lloyd Wright's Vanished Masterpieces*. N.Y.: Simon & Schuster, 1996.

_____. *The Wright Style: Recreating the Spirit of Frank Lloyd Wright*. N.Y.: Simon & Schuster, 1992.

Massey, Anne. *Interior Design of the 20th Century*, World of Art series. London: Thames and Hudson, 1990.

Sommer, Robin L. *Frank Lloyd Wright: A Gatefold Portfolio*. N.Y.: Barnes & Noble Books, 1997.

Spencer, Dorothy. *Total Design: Objects by Architects*. S.F.: Chronicle Books, 1991.

Storrer, Wlliam Allin. *The Architecture of Frank Lloyd Wright: A Complete Catalog*, 2nd ed. Cambridge, Mass.: The MIT Press, 1978.

Wright, Frank Lloyd. *An Autobiography*, 3rd ed. N.Y.: Duell, Sloan and Pearce, 1943.

_____. "In the Cause of Architecture," *Arch. Record* 23 (Mar. 1908).

_____. *The Japanese Print*, 1917; Horizon Press (N.Y.) reprint, 1967.

INDEX